EMBRACING BIODIVERSITY

A SOLUTION TO CLIMATE CHANGE

DANIEL UWITONZE

EMBRACING BIODIVERSITY

A SOLUTION TO CLIMATE CHANGE

DANIEL UWITONZE

If human beings do not pay attention to their actions towards biodiversity, it will cause climate change to increase, and that in itself means the end of the world.

Copyright

Copyright © 2022 Daniel UWITONZE

All rights reserved. No part of this book may be reproduced or used in any manner without the prior written permission of the copyright owner, except for the use of brief quotations in a book review.

To request permissions, contact the Author at danieluwitonze7@gmail.com.

EBook and Paperback edition September 2022

Edited by: Daniel UWITONZE
Cover art by: Daniel UWITONZE
Layout by: Daniel UWITONZE

Dedication

To anyone who thinks of how to protect the future by paying attention to his present actions; and do everything to prevent climate change from increasing.

TABLE OF CONTENTS

DANIEL UWITONZE

INTRODUCTION

Biodiversity is what makes humans last on earth. Conflict and destruction of human toward biodiversity are what will end the world. It is not rocket science to say that a long time will pass until the earth that exists today will have an end because of climate change. The Bible makes it very clear that we will wear another body; Even this world will end, and there comes a new one. And because all changes are related to factors, some factors indicate that some changes may occur as time passes. Think about the effects of nuclear weapons and climate changes.

The first person fled the parts he was in due to changes such as the earth's heat that he could not tolerate, so he found a place to escape and live comfortably. Consider that today the temperature is increasing, and wars using nuclear bombs are going on; this can cause the world to turn into chaos, which the Bible calls the end of the world.

Let me start with the trigger for the point I will talk about in this chapter. At a very young age, during the day I and my brothers and friends looked up at the sky at noon and enjoyed seeing the blue sky. Then, at night we enjoyed going out and looking at the sky and seeing a lot of stars that fit the atmosphere all over the place we could see with our naked eyes.

The rainfall was constant in its time, and the sun had to appear, so rain and sun did not disappoint farmers and ranchers to increase productivity. However, shortly afterward, things changed in the sky, and I started not seeing it as before; the blue sky and the stars were not all over it. I could not see both blue sky and stars as early because the cloud was covering them, the weather changed, and the yield decreased. I wish we could think about it more and not make mistakes again.

God has given us control over everything to sustain us, and now we are destroying our livelihoods, which will negatively affect us in the future. Environmental degradation and climate change were of great concern to human life in the past, today, and the future, yet the human being himself plays a significant role in all these changes. People are in a difficult situation and are at the forefront of actions that will negatively affect them, which will continue to impact them in the future severely. It is as if people were attacked and lost help because we are the ones who attacked ourselves.

The world we have been given contains all the essentials that benefit us differently, but we want more than what we need in the changes we have begun. So as we try to cope with these changes, they push us to bring about other changes that will eventually destroy us. It is as if we have already accepted the corrupted world and continue to plan for self-indulgence. However, if we are not careful about what we do, we will always be in a position to correct our consistent and repetitive mistakes.

Much work has been done on development that will affect us, as evidenced by the history of past actions harming us today, and we have failed to liberate ourselves. For instance, the environment that has been damaged by two world wars, forests that have been cleared for housing, carpentry, and agriculture but now have changed seasons into severe consequences today. Imagine we are drying up wetlands and cutting down forests and rivers for our benefit, which is only for a short time. Indeed we must be prepared and wait for the following kind of punishment while we are still alive or for centuries to come.

Many activities have immediate benefits yet hide the long-term effects on the future. In this century, we are dealing with the impact of climate change, the lack of moderate rainfall, and its appearance when we are not prepared for it. The sun spends a long time damaging the plants until a particular area turns into a desert. Many animals and plants have disappeared, and others are on the verge of extinction. We are concerned about the rising rate of global warming due to the deterioration of the filter that protects us from the sun's rays. The places very close to the sea are slowly melting due to the dense population and man's activities built there with heavy houses. Many serious illnesses are rising and killing many. All these changes make humans more anxious about the future, yet they are more likely to be self-destructive.

We are confused with saving money and storing food as the answer to better long-term health. This is a good thing; however, we should be different from the people who want the well-being of our times to ignore our future and our descendants. After all, the changes we are making to the environment would have pushed us to stop giving birth because we are giving birth in the changed world and keep changing it. Indeed, it will be complicated for our children because they will die from the effects of our lack of discernment, yet we have a way to fix it at the moment. Therefore, people need to stop being selfish and ignoring our offspring because the present people are a practical example of living a threatening and challenging life because of the negligence of some of our predecessors.

A human being is also on the verge of selfishness with no other move than to fall to the ground and break down when they are not well-behaved to learn to at least stay on top of that. In the network of other living things, humankind has shown itself to be self-sufficient and selfish. This has made it difficult for other creatures to survive because of a person's arrogant activities to the point that some creatures have gone extinct.

Know that at all times, other living beings have cases that can accuse people before the Supreme Creator. People posed a severe threat to their everyday lives only as the days passed because what they destroyed and harmed was essential to them. Unfortunately, some of those threats are irreplaceable, and eventually, we began/begin to fear living in our irreversible mistakes.

If we do not change, people still intend to keep destructive actions in the world. In an unthinkable way, but centuries ago, a person's brutality created a great war with other living beings. A person poses a danger to plants and animals, and if possible that for all plants and animals to revenge together for a person, this may be a tragedy that we can never escape. The good thing is that they do not have such selfish behaviors in the ecosystem as humans but seemingly in retaliation for the natural consequences we face. Think carefully about how to control the impact of the work you are going to do on the environment.

We have done some to save the other living things; we left what we called the complex and risky life in the jungle. It was also due to the significant changes we caused, and we could not tolerate them; for this, we built houses to be our new home to escape and cope with those changes. Later, we went back to the forest to hunt animals we had left behind for our food; we burned forests for habitation, besieged what was left; then we fled to our new homes; we felt it was enough.

If it is understandable that a person has escaped a difficult life in the jungle due to severe environmental degradation, the one used the wisdom of building a house away from the forest to be one's shelter and refuge. After all, a person knows how to defend oneself to survive, and in any case, humankind will strive to be the last to remain on earth by sacrificing other living things so that we may not perish. It is good to know why God created us and an environment full of other living creatures. Because it's important to humans, the creation of diversity was to bring enough human resources for his sustenance. Proper management is what is needed to keep us alive without losing anything.

The world and everything in it is the gift given to us to control and manage; what would be the explanations if God asked us how we handled the shared natural resources? Reflect on the reasons behind your creation and your responsibilities in the world. When you look at the damage caused by human activities, it is a significant sign that a human being is the most endangered species in the world compared with other living things.

It is supposed that God's creation should feed us, but we do it self-destructively. To survive, we must destroy the environment. People are accustomed to defending and satisfying themselves without caring about the lives of other living things. Reflecting on this and the reason for the action would help us control and adequately manage other creatures instead of destroying them.

Don't you see that everything God created is essential? If you need help to understanding it correctly, you should sit down and think about each one and know its importance. What you call a terrible creature is very important in a logical way for your benefit, So God created each of them in a way that sustains human beings. Understandably, warfare between other living beings is beneficial to humans as the most valuable creatures in front of God.

Naturally, a cat can be prey to a dog, and a mouse can be prey to a cat so that every living organism can be food to each other. All of this food chain does not harm the environment and often ends up being beneficial to human beings. Hunting or fights among animals themselves do not abuse the environment; instead, it's a natural mechanism for ecosystem balance. However, it becomes terrible when humans intervene. God is fantastic because He created the predators and gave them the innate ability to hunt and find prey. A God also gave the target the ability to hide from the predators and defend themselves during the hunt.

Don't you see God created everything in an unchanging and well-built system to love and bless us humans? Now look at the water that starts life for green plants, and God allows plants to have an unchanging system of life to exist but to be the beginning of the food chain for all other living things. The CO_2 we usually take as lousy air, yet it is helpful for plants to make its nutrients for growth; Green plants become a food source for other living organisms. Besides being food for grass-eating animals (herbivorous), it provides good air O_2 to humans and other animals for respiration. The previous statement explains how a person should accept and digest the bad things that happen to him and all the good things which come, and then a person has to consider them all as they are there to make a living. No matter all the bad things you have received, you should give out good things to others just as plants accept bad air (CO2) and give good air (O2); this would be a positive principle to follow.

To stop the damage, you need to know the origin of everything and know that for green plants to exist requires water and sun at an average rate without dominance in either one of them. When the sun dominates, the plants will dry up, and when the rain becomes too heavy, the plants will float through the flood, and soil erosion may occur. All will occur in moderation only if human activities align with environmental conservation, and this will be a sustainable solution to the food chain system. Thus it is time for us people to stop behaving as if we do not need to live a life and stop making actions that destroy our life and contradict the creator's wishes.

It is not necessary that if you need fish, then you have to kill all the fish without separating young from old fish. It is a shameful and suicidal decision to satisfy our current needs, yet the result will make us face the catastrophe we've caused ourselves. It is also important not to cut down forests to find a place to build a prosperous shining city, and yet you ignore the life of urban dwellers that will be affected by the polluted air due to cutting down trees. After all, the world needs green cities, not shining and bright cities.

Considering how fast we are harming the environment and living things but still rarely going together to find a solution, you might think that we want to be distinct or that other organisms need us more than we need them. Instead, we betray ourselves because other living things may exist in our absence. Imagine when we will reduce the fish in livers, seas, and oceans in contrast to what it is now, and then think of those who will get the fish and their ability and how the poor will live. That time the health inequality will be high, and the poor will be worse off. True humanity reflects the cause and effect of any action intended to protect the future of our planet.

Of course and where possible, the natural energy and a lifestyle that is characterized by eating raw foods will save the world. The natural state of things does not cause harm but instead begins to be wrong when human intelligence deviates and changes. All start with people's internal arguments like: "Let us change it in this way, this is how it should be, but this is not very good, and let's change it," and then we hastily say it and do it without analyzing the consequences and blinding ourselves to its immediate and obvious benefits.

However, as we change it, it also changes with its nature that was important to us before. Sometimes, changes like these bring other changes to the point that they affect the lives of plants and animals, which has to affect humankind automatically. Above all, we must protect animals and plants because we know their importance in people's health. But, unfortunately, the more we think we are developing intelligence, the more we damage the environment, unlike the former people who obeyed the law of the forest, which has resulted in natural conservation.

Compared to the people of that time, they were undeveloped until they developed a fire discovery that helped them eat roasted meat and burn dense forests to make hunting easier. But unfortunately, when a person discovered fire, fire became the beginning of the destruction of the environment, which was also self-destructive. Therefore, the new intelligence we get probably comes with more destruction than the benefits of what we have discovered with our minds.

Fire burns to create something craftily, and fire cooks but also burns and destroys the organisms. The smoke provides also creates a problem in the atmosphere because it damages the sun rays filter that prevents us from global warming. The forests burned down during that time were also extinguished with many possible organisms. The aforementioned raised tons of smoke in the atmosphere and the results were weather deterioration and seasonal changes (natural imbalance). Fire also quickly became a significant weapon in hunting large numbers of animals. It was a surprising, dangerous, and unique weapon that other animals were not used to seeing from their mate human beings while still in the same jungle. Watching the fire on animals was so scary because until now, they still don't understand how to use it and its secret.

Fire immediately helped create new objects intended to protect human beings and keep them safe regardless of any other organisms damaged by fire. But, as the revolution continues, it goes with the changes that endanger the world more than before, and the more it becomes tricky, the more the people strive to create the tool that will help them survive.

The world is getting more challenging and will remain if there is no change. It is due to the severe damage that has resulted in famine, inadequate sun protection, and the high cost of treating severe illnesses caused by these changes, which continue to make the poor more vulnerable. However, in the past years, most people were at the same level of life with little wealth difference. Their dangers were the same and shared; they joined hands to fight them. We can't go back in time, but we could bring it into the image of the time we are in today and make it possible by respecting natural settings.

There are many destructive acts, but some people do them because they do not think about the lives of many and those who will come next to them when they are no longer alive. You should always think about the reason behind all the changes you are seeing and have a clear understanding of why, but also think about the consequences of specific actions you do. We are using our minds to self-destruct; we have reduced our lifespan, caused landslides, stopped the rain in some areas, caused heavy rainfall damage, and damaged the ozone layer, resulting in increased earth heat. We seem to be digging a grave that will bury us when nothing is done to stop this damage. There are times when what we call economic competition instead appears to be competition for the continued deterioration of nature, which will eventually affect us negatively.

You wonder what life will be like in 2050. Maybe in terms of bright and shining cities, we will be doing well, but here I would be grateful if you could consider the extent of environmental degradation we will have in that time. Maybe we will survive 2050, but what will it be like in 2100? I am sure wealthy people will develop technology and lifestyle to help them to live with the effects of those degradations, but how will the poor survive?

Because of your religious beliefs, you may think that the end will come, that the world will end, or that Jesus will have already come; some may say that we will have already died. Still, your loved ones and descendants will remain in the generations after you. However, I strongly agree that we will end this world ourselves at some point if we do not change our attitudes and behavior. So, think about why you are going to do something and think about the consequences.

I thought about this based on the changes I have seen as soon as I became aware of it. I asked elders if they realized the changes as I saw them. They told me so much more that you, too, can read in this book, or you may know more than just what I wrote and make them the points to bring about positive change. Many interviewees did not know what I was saying, but I hope the wise one found my intention. Ultimately, they are aware of the change, and some realize what is happening.

I was born in a rural area, where most of what I saw was natural at the time. It was very likely different from what it was before I was born because I was the future they had heard about! The existing infrastructure seemed to be the unpaved roads, and we were sitting in the round woods at the schools. Many have changed due to the nation's development as the reason for good governance. That emphasizes the positive changes we can make in the world and make it possible.

Those changes have brought about the extinction of some wildlife, soil erosion, and rivers and lakes drying up. Still, they have also brought about invisible creatures that can cope with environmental degradation. Some of these organisms may live in the body of another organism as a human being and cause serious illnesses, and epidemics increase. After all, humans are not the only ones who know how to make a living. Remember that other living things may live in our bodies and that we will die with some and leave another. We seem to be standing in the negative consequences of what we have done to ourselves, yet a person is at the forefront of the causes of change that profoundly affect human beings.

Of course, there are new epidemics that we think are not common, yet the insects that cause these diseases have already existed. As the years go by, because of their defenses, they can cope with climate change and adopt more power and the ability to cause more severe illnesses than ever before. You may have heard of epidemics such as measles, mumps, and other outbreaks of the same disease. These epidemics killed more people than those killed by the war; sadly, these are products of humans through our mistakes.

THE PURPOSE OF GOD BY CREATING BIODIVERSITY

Ecosystems are made up of a lot of diversity, which has important implications for the health of all living things; Humans should recognize the critical value of each element in the ecosystem, and none should be underestimated. I am always amazed at the system God put in place when He first created the most vital thing in giving life. That is light, water, and air, and although they give life, God did not provide them with life so that they would not die; their absence would cease life. To destroy that is an unforgettable destruction in the history of human activities.

To understand it clearly, the combination of these three is where the life of the first organism came from, and even today, producers in the food chain make their own food from that combination; you will come to understand it better as you keep reading the book. You should know that every living thing is made up of more water than other things. For instance, a person is composed of 60%, fish is about 80%, and the plant is above 80%; it is not even possible for food to exist without water. So if you pollute the water, you will be killing yourself.

The reason why life still exists is that the combination of the above still exists. Another thing is that for living things to be called breathers is because they use air; and contamination of the air will stop breathing, and where there is no air, be it oxygen or carbon dioxide, there will be no life. The same is true of light, which gives life when it combines with air (carbon dioxide) and water, making green living things synthesize their own food as producers.

Water needs air as air needs water, and they need light as light needs air and water; I mean, all living things need water, air, and sunlight. So let it be clear because animals or plants will not read this book; they do not harm the environment, but you as a person should know that you and your friends (other creatures) need water, air, and sunlight, and in an average way because that is what conserves the nature.

People should know that we don't need too much sun because it is harmful; we don't need more rain to destroy. Hey, we don't even need much carbon dioxide, though we are almost always cutting down the forests. We need all of them reasonably constant; this concept shows that we should always look for actions that can be taken to reach conservation.

If it requires us to plant forests, do it; if it requires us to stop wars, do it because they themselves pollute the air and water, and the harmful gases will damage the solar filter and end up with Global warming. I do not doubt that starting a war will not save any of that. Cutting down and burning forests will not help us, and massive and unreasonable consumption of natural resources by exploitation will not help us in conservation. Humans have become destroyers instead of being the protectors of the ecosystem, which poses us with both short-term and long-term consequences.

The principle of diversity that allows for nature conservation is the food chain; the food chain is a series of organisms that get food from producers, followed by primary consumers, then secondary and tertiary consumers, and finally, consumers. This results in some organisms dying and others being born, and the cycle continues. To understand it better, you should know that after producers, one organism eats another to survive, which does not harm nature.

In living things, there are predators and prey, and one has its predator and prey; it's like a life full of attention, so you don't become a victim. God is unique because He gave predators the ability to hunt and gave prey a way to hide from predators, so they don't become prey. So in such a system, it is always necessary for the predator not to be lazy to hunt; also, the target is required to be careful so that they do not die and disappear.

This is what happens in biodiversity, you will find that the mice eat plants and snacks, but mice are also prey for predators called cats, and finally, cats become the prey of dogs, and this cycle does not make mice or cats disappear, but it is nature conservation. In this series, man is the final consumer and the strong predator.

In general, other animals do not kill prey when they do not want to eat, but a person is very destructive to one's sustenance because a person kills and destroys what one does not want to eat without any apparent reason. Nature conservation benefits humans, but one becomes the first to destroy nature more than any other living thing. Some people are so intoxicated by killing that they kill various other creatures until they don't think much about the consequences of what they harm; they continue to have an addiction to killing until they kill other people.

Usually, a predator can kill prey for food; this means that animals in the same species do not kill each other as often as humans do. Apart from the food chain, be aware that wherever you see dead animals, you will often find them killed by humans or their blind actions. Sadly, we see people dying all the time, yet rarely will you find someone killed by an animal, only by people; this often means that if you find a dead animal or person, they were probably killed by people or their unreasonable actions.

Among other living creatures, a person is only a creature that does not tolerate differences, so one's actions harm different organisms to the point where one sees another who is different as a person who does not deserve to exist.

To understand the brutality of damaged humankind and to know how strong and dangerous a predator we are, Note that we usually hide not from other animals but from humans. That is what happens when a person says to themself, "Let me protect a thief from entering my house," or "Let me protect myself from a killer coming into my house." Even the animals know how bad we are because they cannot walk in daylight because they fear a strong predator, humankind. So it is; many animals cover themselves at night so that man does not kill them; that's why they run away or decide to fight when they see someone.

The fact that humans belong to the animal kingdom does not itself make us animals in nature and behavior. A man who kills a fellow human is clothed with cruelty, and other animals should surely be afraid of that person.

If you have heard about a peace mission in a particular country by UN forces or from other countries, I tell you the truth that they are going to protect people from being killed by other people, I mean terrorists. When it comes to the practices of destroying the environment, you cannot compare humans to other living things. I continue to explain that being human means having humanity, and humanity is thinking about what is good for you and other people and all the things around you.

We should show our kindness to other creatures and at least offer a positive difference. Still, it isn't easy because we are even losing humanity to our fellow human beings. Still, some people are cruel like animals and have become terrible animals to people and other creatures. It is not interesting at all, and it does not help the ecosystem that there are strong predators among people, causing some to become like their prey. That is when life becomes a never-ending hunt and hide; then brutality overwhelms humanity. This behavior causes people to harm other living things in large numbers when hunting their fellow creatures to kill them.

Humans should not be unreasoning predators to the extent that they disrupt other people's peace to show them that they are strong. These actions push people into many irreparable mistakes of destroying plants such as forests, polluting air and water, and sending harmful gases into the atmosphere that destroy the ozone layer. So after killing our fellow citizens, we are left with harmful effects such as global warming, breathing bad air, life-threatening water pollution, lack of food due to drought, and many more that I cannot list right now.

Lucky for us humans is that God continues to give prey the ability to hide and God does not allow predators to multiply to extent of overwhelming the prey because the world would end. Humans should indeed think about our role in the ecosystem because we are the species that have the intelligence to control its destruction. Still, instead, we are doing the opposite and destroying ourselves. Our diversity in biodiversity exists to help us to preserve the environment.

They say that no one is enough alone, and this is true. Above, we saw the lesson of how one food is not enough to provide a complete diet for a person. Instead, how they unite from different species and each one plays its role is what gives a balanced diet.

Biodiversity is an adventure; imagine If life is characterized by being in one place, eating the same things, seeing only one color, and seeing the same people all the time, it would stress you out. This approach would make you lack some knowledge so that if you live for a long time in such a way of life, it will cause problems when you move to another unfamiliar place. After all, always looking at the same thing that doesn't change will damage your mind.

After all, a diet consisting of only one kind of substance is useless because it is not enough alone. Instead, eating a variety of foods is more effective because they include bodybuilding, disease-fighting, and energy-boosting foods.

We all know that eggs are good for building the body because they are made up of protein. Eating them is good, but whenever a person eats them alone, it will have negative effects, including obesity. Again, sugar gives you energy, but it's not good enough because it can cause diabetes mellitus. Incredibly, even the fruits and vegetables that prevent diseases must be combined with other foods to be effective. All this happens because you don't need to eat energy-giving foods only and forget to eat bodybuilding foods. After all, a weak body is not productive; a sick body is useless. They are all helpful when combined; they provide a balanced diet. No creature is enough alone.

In diversity, nothing is more valuable than another in terms of giving life; the problem is that we don't know how to use disparities successfully. Biodiversity provides many different, but each of them has its own importance. For example, one should realize that a person does not need only meat; one needs it on average and combined with other different foods. Understanding this makes us avoid killing animals and instead raise them as the source of meat for generations. Well, loving one thing in diversity also destroys, but respecting each one for its contribution to life is necessary because nothing created by God is useless.

Referring to the example of preferring meat over other foods, this in itself would cause many animals to be killed and lost. Also, eating meat often causes gout, which is why I said above that the love of only one thing is worthless. On the other hand, there is nothing that one should reject in biodiversity because it itself brings death. Still, a person started the damage due to a lack of wisdom until the difference brought conflict among them.

HUMAN'S DUTIES TOWARD BIODIVERSITY

In the time of living thing creation, autotrophic-based organisms were made before others; this is because they produce oxygen, so this oxygen is what is consumed by all the other organisms that were made after. Human being had to wait for the creation of other organisms, like plants, that would sustain them. After all, God created man because everything was created first to feed him, and person to control them.

The above point explains why human beings should have respect for other living things because they depend on them for their livelihood. After the existence of other living things, we saw that man came into existence later, and everything to be created went through an inevitable process to come into existence.

The fact that the world is made up of many diverse organisms made God creates man to manage and control everything in the world; even because people are different from each other, that is why one of them leads them to a particular area. And because the world and the universe have many differences, there is a God who guides and controls everything.

God has given you the inner guidance to control everything around you so you can live without harming others. Your works have to be good while alive, and your work should have a good effect in the future. Dominion and leadership of human does not mean that one should consider other organisms of lesser value in the ecosystem, but to understand that people live because of other living things that feed people.

In short, we exist because other creatures exist, without which man would not exist. Therefore, Dominion and leadership should not be against other living things but have them by using wisdom to plan a better life for others thousands of years in the future.

God created you to rule, manage, and control everything in the world, Genesis Chapter 1verse 26. He has made you a wise living creature in all other beings; you exist to govern yourself and, in particular, to manage and control other living beings around you. God knows that His creation is sufficient to sustain man; God has been able to provide for Adam with all which feeds him, including many kinds of fruits, animals of the earth, animals in the water, and birds. I always wonder what the explanation would be for God if He asked us how we managed the gift of the world we were given!

In this ecosystem, the well-being of everyone should come from the perfect relationship between a man and His surroundings. Therefore, to live a good life as God intended, He has asked a person to control all the rest of creation so that there will be no loss of human sustenance in the future.

God also had another purpose in creating you: to govern every part of the earth, from the sea, land, and sky. Remember that to lead is not to destroy and misuse, but to proper management, because in what God has given us to lead, we find our food; Genesis 1:29.

Naturally, we know that when a person is in charge, he should always look for something that will improve their subordinates. However, in the case of Dominion that God gave the people, He wanted to show them that there is no other creature as intelligent as humans, the reason that should make humans lead other animals and plants as well.

And the indicated also means that no animal should reach the point where they may harm a human being, and they should not be few for a human being because it is in the living being that God has placed our food. It means that the more we risk their lives, the more difficult it will be for our life, and the more we will not be able to cope with the misery we have brought. The less time it will take for others living to perish, the more we will be in danger. Relationships between humans and other creatures should be characterized by mutual respect instead of harm.

A person as a leader should have a vision and think about other living things because their existence in a controlled way is the existence of a human being. The rest is a mistake of cutting the branch of a tree that we sit at, and it is like inserting pieces of wood in the spring from a well that feeds us. We all know that plants do not think about the future, and we control their lives because we are the ones who decide what to eat and what helps us in our daily lives.

Everything started with their originality until they changed because of the poor management of the person, and it goes on and on until we find that it is hard to correct that mistake. When natural power fails, we begin excessively harvesting crops to fill the void we have already caused. Instead of controlling and ruling our sustenance, we created damage to our nature, and now we entered into the reformation of every creature.

So human sustenance has started to be low; we are losing meat, we are missing vegetables, we are missing cereals, and simply we are missing out on food. Therefore, to reverse this catastrophe, many living beings are being forced to reproduce and produce a yield that is too high to satisfy the market through artificial farming. While we continue to put in all this form of effort, it will not solve the problems caused by our mismanagement of what we have been given because even as we do, this poverty continues to increase. Many die of starvation because our livelihoods often cost so much that the poor cannot afford it.

It is even more likely that the methods we use to close the gap will be detrimental and will significantly impact human development in the future. If we keep failing to control what God has given us the ability to control, it will end up creating what controls us instead of controlling them, especially for the poor, who will be in more danger than the wealthy people.

It is clear from the above explanation that we have failed to manage the natural resources given to us by the Creator. However, the high demand for some of the world's products poses a serious threat to our planet; this brings climate change due to industrial emissions and eventually causes droughts all over the earth. Moreover, mismanagement has a detrimental effect on our health. Therefore, thinking about it allows us to take care of our management to keep plants, birds, land animals, and aquatic animals alive and well and to think about their welfare for our future.

Of course, one must think about the birds and know their species and way of life so that none of them will disappear. No creature is of no value to the person when it is properly controlled as God has ordained. We need to be aware of what birds eat so we do not harm their livelihoods. Even more, pandemics occur because we may have killed the organism that should have protected us. Some organisms that cause the epidemic may no longer have a place to live other than humans due to our environmental degradation.

Humans are powerful beings who can think about the future until we think about it for centuries. The most intelligent person is the one who thinks about the future in the long run. This kind of thinking requires us to think about the life of other living organisms and the protection of our surroundings.

Above all, we live as a result of the good or bad effects of our actions or those of our predecessors. What they have done well, in the long run, has a positive impact on us today, and what they have done poorly harms us today. It means that every generation has left a mark on what has been done well or badly. Therefore, we should think about the future and also corrects some of the mistakes that our predecessors made.

Sadly, we are changing the world, yet we will regret it for years to come because it will have a devastating effect on our descendants and us. Therefore, self-control and proper control of every creature is our absolute responsibility because the more we do it, the more time we have for living and our descendants. So we have to be careful in what we do so that we will not live to correct the mistakes that have been made and we will not have to deal with the brutal and negative consequences which will also affect our future generations.

Think about the reasons behind what we see today and how we do it today, knowing that they will impact the future. Ignoring the reason for your creation and the power God has given you seems to be a failure of self-control, and this is the end of your life, especially to your descendants, when no severe and long-term actions are taken.

Ignoring biodiversity leads us to the mistake of destroying the environment. Humans know we are incredible creatures, but that doesn't make us forget other creatures with great value in making our lives exist.

A wise person is a person who understands the source of what one owns, so s/he protects it and preserves it. Our human behavior should always consider the importance of other living things; this will make us take care of our harmful everyday activities.

ORIGIN OF BIODIVERSY AND ITS CONNECTION WITH HUMAN BEING

Whatever you can explain about the existence of life, you can't end without talking about supernatural power; that is a perfect point that connects God with creation. The connection of too many different things is what gave life. Therefore, no single substance by itself can give life because every reaction requires a combination of various substances to form the desired product.

Biodiversity is God's purpose, and everything God created has its diversity, and God was happy because of the intention of creating life. After all, variety begins with the creation of the world and the universe. God created everything differently because it pleased Him, and in order to emphasize the difference, He created everything on different days.

This is how God created the universe, and on the first day, God created light, and God saw that it was good. On the second day, God created the universe, which He called the sky, and He also looked at the different systems of the universe and found them to be good. Then, God created the sea, land, and plants as diverse as their species, which he made on the third day, and he is also pleased with that diversity.

God created the sun, the moon, and the stars to rule the day and night and remind people of the seasons and years when the fourth day is over. And on the fifth day, God created all living things, those in the water, on the earth, and flying in the air as their species are, and he created them from the dust. So He ended on the sixth day by creating man and woman from the dust. So on the seventh day, he rested because he was happy with what He made that filled the world and the universe; and God was proud of the man who was created to control the world's contents. You will read the Bible Genesis 1:1-27. Surprisingly, God created many different things; as God created different things, He saw them as good things to please Him.

Since ancient times, biodiversity has given life to man. The new thing that a person discovered was different from the previous one, and that discovery was to provide a human being with a better life. The big bang is believed to be the explosion that gave rise to the smallest particles that make up every kind of life in the universe. This explosion created a universe of many systems I cannot explain.

That same universe has various systems, including the solar system; that solar system is where the blue planet is located. This world is surrounded by water and air in the atmosphere, which becomes the source of life for living things. The simplest way to understand it, was that the explosion of a single object, like a hot ball, resulted in many different things that gave rise to life. Very quickly, history shows that intelligent man (Homo sapiens) appeared in the East African highlands in the last two hundred thousand years.

His lifestyle was characterized by living with biodiversity in the middle of the forest. His food came from hunting, so he ate the meat of various animals. So that place in the jungle became a hiding place for him. As he became wise, he discovered a fire that helped him eat roasted meat and light at night, and he used it for hunting and making weapons and other tools.

The light has given someone the idea of starting the search and discovering many different things. Curiosity made a person discover new things to this day; it ended someone found how to cultivate, bringing a variety of food rather than eating meat only. As He kept finding different things, he fled the forest where he built a house to be home, even a resting place for forest injury. He and his friends continued the journey to discover various parts of the World and increase the world population in different areas.

The connection is this; the Bible reveals that after God brought all living things to Adam to name them, he also called them according to their species. It makes sense that Adam didn't do that in one day, but it took him time to explore every living thing. Another thing is that all the animals had females, and Adam did not have a wife yet.

So he was exhausted even after looking at the male and female of every kind of animal; God gave him a helper and called her a woman. This made Adam the first explorer and researcher who could name all living things. Otherwise, the world would have left us with an ecosystem without names, although there is no shortage of answers for humans.

Research is something that continues, and at that time, the art of writing did not come as a classification of everything in a documented way. As the world progressed, the explorers discovered and wrote down everything we know today, they left us with a beautiful legacy, and they did it well. Philosophers have used the popular philosophy of questioning everything. They say "why this?" and that so that they know the structure and function of each one and see how they do the classification.

Yes, everything starts with the living being and non-living things; non-living things are all things that do not breathe but help start life. That is why God created light, air, and water before anything else. Everything that begins life is what was created before everything else. Many non-living things are classified into many categories, from artificial to natural non-living things. However, they all exist in different forms to play separate roles in life-giving.

It means that anything that does not give life is useless and should not even be given a place in biodiversity. However, all that is useless comes from man-made things and not from God. Among them are the weapons of war, and they are made and given great value in life, but they are from the conflict of not knowing the mission of diversity. They make them and kill their fellows (people) because there is something they differ from. Unfortunately, it ends up damaging the environment.

The fact that biodiversity exists means that there are differences, but the first thing is that there is a common denominator. For instance, Living things include many species, but the common denominator is that they all breathe. Researchers show that living things should at least be classified into seven classifications in descending order from the most significant class to the point where humans are different from other living things.

The classification includes Kingdom, phylum, class, order, family, Genus, and species. Let's take an example from people; we are in the Kingdom of Animalia, which includes all animals that move and eat other living things to survive, just to list few traits. The human phylum is chordate/vertebrate, which means all vertebrates belong to the same phylum as humans. The class is mammals, all animals with breasts and lactating. The order is the primate, which includes monkeys. The family is Homonidae. The fifth is homo Linnaeus, the Genus; the species is Homo sapiens, the modern intelligent man.

In an ecosystem, nothing should interfere with another. Because we are all Homo sapiens, we should understand and respect each other because we are the same. And people should respect other organisms because they include those that belong to the same Genus, others to family, order, class, phylum, and all the animals that belong to the Kingdom of Animalia. The most important thing is that among the five kingdoms in the world are Animalia, Plantae, Fungi, Protoctista, and prokaryotes, but all are included in living things.

Yes, there are differences but they are associated with the importance of each organism in the ecosystem. Still, the links between organisms are so many that they should be valued to make the world a better place. If you look carefully and know the value of a specific animal, you will not abuse it again. If you know the importance of plants, you will start to preserve the environment with interest.

Once you know the importance of bacteria, you will understand that there are bacteria that are important in the ecosystem. No living thing is without significance in ecosystem health and balance. The problem is that we misuse the distinction.

HUMAN ACTIVITIES IN ENVIRONMENT POLLUTION AND CLIMATE CHANGES

CONFLICTS AND WARS

Looking at the pace and intensity of the bombings and looking at the lost budget, you may think that they are making bread for the people of the world when famine strikes or when problems arise that require staying home (Lockdown) as COVID-19 did. Yet it is all about killing people, not only killing the people destroying territory, country, and continent. In addition, it all ends up polluting the air, starving everyone from destroying and damaging human resources, which will have a lasting impact on the lives of all living things. So let me say out loud, "It is to rush to do things that end up ruining yourself without leaving others, and this has no wisdom."

The idea is that humans do this by making nuclear bombs, not to attack aliens or other tragedies that would invade the earth or a particular part of it, but these bombs are for destroying humans themselves. The bombs, however, do not kill anyone because they are often with the intended targets, destroying infrastructure and destroying mountains, valleys, forests, and other wildlife habitats.

Bombing will also increase the amount of smoke that pollutes the atmosphere; the survivors of these destructive weapons will live a complicated life in the face of the resulting global warming. When they make these bombs, they think of a bit of damage to the air they breathe after defeating the so-called enemy.

In the battleground of these dangerous weapons, you will find that they wear some of the coverings so that they are not affected by the bombs they use. It is because they are not afraid to use poison bombs to destroy their opponents, and because they know the evils of the weapons, they wear masks, covering their eyes and noses to breathe fresh air.

Also, once they kill people, they damage other living things, creating something new that will be bad in the years to come. This is because the poison that infiltrated the survivor will cause so much damage that will reduce expected production, and the rest is to die due to the poison that had entered the person.

The war pollutes the environment like forests and other natural vegetation that are important for the use of the bad air we breathe, and they give us the fresh air we breathe. Here, it causes the air to be polluted by fumes constantly circulating as nuclear bombs damage forests and other plants. A survivor will suffer from many respiratory illnesses due to a lack of fresh air but will also breathe bad breath from toxic explosives.

This case of respiratory diseases and the emergence and evolution of insect-borne insects will be on the rise. In a few days, new epidemics begin to devastate the masses who have escaped the war of gunfire and bombing. Not only that, wars cause animals to migrate to the place where they meet or live with humans and infect them with animal-borne diseases and epidemics like influenza of all kinds and rabies; the world will be in greater danger than war itself.

Nor can we ignore the deterioration of water and its biodiversity due to explosive or toxic substances. That makes the water lose its usefulness and is useless in all respects, like drinking, cooking, and not used for irrigation of crops. The organisms in damaged water begin to die trying to live in unfamiliar places.

Wars also bring the displacement of people from their homes to living in difficult conditions in forests and new camps that are either functional or intended for them. This can lead to a densely populated place with minimal hygienic requirements. That can lead to the development of contagious diseases and the rapid spread of epidemics. Also, due to the large number of people who are going to live in one place, there is an exploitation of resources which ends up harming the environment.

To provoke war by seeking power in other countries, to provoke it by cruelty, brutality, and hatred, or with the intention of revenge is not Humanity. Stop this because its benefits are minimal compared to the consequences of war today and in the future. If they say there is nothing good about war, you have to understand the loss of human lives and the destruction of the environment. , hear a lot about the consequences that will befall the future of Humanity.

If we believe that the world is our house, then our house is our home and our descendants, so why do we destroy and severely damage our home? There is no reason to create war, yet we ignore the consequences of the environmental degradation of the world in which we all live.

We share the atmosphere because its effects come for both of us, and we share it when the damage happens. The heavy bombs you make to kill the enemy don't even leave the atmosphere and sky blue as it was, so start preparing to deal with climate change in a way you won't be able to overcome due to your brutality and negative thoughts of your mind. If we are smart enough, we should get out of our homes and come together to see if we can make weapons that stop the rise in temperature and the rate of famine in certain parts of the world. Let's go together and see if there is a peaceful weapon that will stop a particular animal from disappearing and becoming extinct.

We intend to hear those from the resolutions of the UN General Assembly, the White House, the Kremlin, and other respected national and international organizations. The good decisions they make, then the people we should be ready to implement. As I mentioned above, the human brain has been creating many new things since the discovery of fire. The creation of new ones will destroy all human species after other living things are completed.

Here, people have lighted the fire to the extent that they have brought it among themselves. Do you wonder about what happened in the first and second world wars? What if a Third one comes? Can you imagine how harmful it can be due to what we call human intelligence development?

I hear many people talk about money as compensation for the damage. Still, none can pay for the millions of dead people or animals and plants lost, the air damage, or the damage done after severe damage from the number of pollutants emitted in the atmosphere. I don't think that is worth the money we give them. Eventually, the people who won the war invented it and started it among themselves. They are killing each other and destroying the future of humans and living things. Intelligence development has led people to a great race that turned into a battle to the level of starting a war. It seems that the most intelligent people are those who strive for themselves and stop others from getting such knowledge and do so in a serious way to create an apparent war. Some fight so that tomorrow there will be no substitute for possessing nuclear weapons; they want to be the first to endanger the world.

After all, saving for the future should not only be money, but it should also be to reduce the damage to the world because money cannot return to the world as it once was before. Therefore, saving for children should not only protect them from abusers or save money for them in the future but also correct the mistakes we make that will harm the future of our children and their descendants.

So saving the world is more than just stopping the dead and rejoicing that it is over, but remembering the damage that can cause many deaths in the future. A genuinely wise person is well-prepared for the future of their descendants and invests in their education. In that case, they should remember the most important environmental protection measures because it is also a source of well-being for the children.

DEVELOPMENT AND ECONOMICS ACTIVITIES

Destroying the world has been the cost of development in many countries. Developed and developing countries are polluting the air, water, and land. They are all used exhaustively, and the soil produces all the expected yields in the form of exploitation, use of water for other purposes such as providing more energy than usual, and human activities severely pollute the air.

If they talk about developed countries, you will immediately understand the role of those countries in environmental degradation. Hear tons of carbon dioxide emissions, tons of waste from their development activities, and the damage to water and its ecosystems. However, on the other hand, it is often the case that underdeveloped countries are at the bottom of the list and are often asked to continue to do so. How do you think the world would be damaged if all the countries were like China or the United States, or if most of them found themselves at the same pace of development as Brazil and India? I tell you the truth; we would set fire to the Earth.

The effort we put into developing industries should go alongside activities to conserve and preserve the environment.

Nature conservation should go hand in hand with any development project in any country. After all, development without fresh air O2 damages the water and its contents, which sustain us; this will cause us to die without eating what we are tired of. In some analyses, development has reduced the lifespan of our lives in general. Here it is better to consider the concept of each development activity in terms of health protection; we may find a few basic ones that will keep our lives and their hopes for our descendants. Don't you see, as the world progresses in general, so does the death of the people increase because the killers have become so numerous that everyone is a candidate for death?

The most polluted countries should pay attention to the fact that we share the atmosphere and unlimited winds; these winds help us share everything in the sky. Remember also we have rivers, lakes, and seas that at some point bring to us the results of water pollution that you have made. If you pollute the water and the air will not only affect you but also come up with an effect that you will share with others who have no interest or benefits in your environmental degradation activities. We will share the consequences, but their development will remain at home; this will give your citizens a better quality of life because the weather is terrible for both of us, but growth is only for a certain country. The emphasis on the world will continue to be very difficult for the incompetent.

Think of the fumes raised in two world wars and those from industrialization in many industrialized countries. All of these have added tons of greenhouse gasses that damage the ozone filter, which will inevitably affect us sooner or later in the long run. In addition, industrial smoke in many parts of the world has removed the blue sky, which is now history in many countries.

The future generation will ask about the blue sky and some explanation of many other things lost because of our actions. We are very sorry if we take no action because we are preparing for the world's end. Even if it is for the sake of development, we will only look at it and die because we will not survive for long.

It is good that we are increasing the population, which requires us to destroy forests, rivers, and swamps to find a place to live, yet our damage is irreplaceable. Urbanization is increasing because of the large number of people, and so as people continue to expand the city, the same way they destroy all possibilities for better health.

Often many urban development projects play a significant role in damaging the local environment. Of course, some swamps have changed into our habitat, and we cut down the forests to make a living.

Many development projects are no different from environmental degradation; think of the mining as leaving high mountains, destroying forests, and changing the nature of specific places. Here, it also makes it easier for the rain to flow through the soil to cause erosion, so human life is threatened.

It is not right that if we find minerals or petrol on land or in the water, we should immediately expedite the exploitation without thinking of at least the value of the wealth we want in the ground and water and the life of other living things. Think about this to know what to do at the right time and place. It is good that all infrastructures need to be checked first and foremost based on their benefits and consequences. Our eyes should be wide open to see future effects because the immediate benefits often deceive us, blind us, and lead us to make irreversible mistakes.

When done improperly without considering the consequences and being compared to the benefits that will come from a particular developmental activity, all development ends up causing problems for the Earth's climate and seasons. In any case, the nature of the exploitation is problematic for the future and will inevitably come. There are some we created that we value, yet they are of little value in real life compared to primary human resources because you can live without them.

It is miserable to find someone mining in the mountains, valleys, swamps, and water wells in which you are looking for mineral resources to be used to build nuclear weapons. Imagine exploiting land or water and deforestation for shining and brightening materials in front of you. At the same time, you damaged the soil and left it in the vicinity of those areas, only to be surrounded by the high cost of living that left where the stones came from. Deforestation is also due to construction, carpentry, and good-quality timber from the forest. Imagine damaging water and its ecosystems for some reason without considering the consequences.

Given the current pace of environmental degradation through many development activities, we don't want to live long enough. Therefore, there is a need for detailed consideration of any developmental action before it goes into action. We can consider the following questions, which require us to constantly wonder why each activity and its effects in the foreseeable future. These questions should be like, Why are we going to start this? Is it worth or is it necessary? Can they negatively affect our lives without leaving other living beings? Doesn't it harm the environment? What are the benefits or disadvantages to human health in general? The better answer should be to make a healthy decision that we will have no regret in the future.

Research has shown that our world has changed, which is true because you can see it with your own eyes; obviously, its natural structure has changed dramatically. Genuinely, after the world's creation, the first man did not find roads, no buildings, and no great technology like today. So much has changed, and no doubt that if our forefathers may have returned, they might be surprised by seeing tremendous changes. That also brought climate change rooted in the drying up of the oceans, rivers, wetlands, and streams and the clearing of forests and wetlands.

The world has continued to change to the point of extinction of some plants and organisms because some could no longer withstand the changes. Imagine when our ancestors return to life; they would find a devastated world where even staying just for one second is not easy for them due to the change that took place.

Still, I always wonder what the explanation would be for God if He asked us how we managed the gift of the world given! Think about how good it was before and how it would be great if you could think about your contribution to preventing some of the things you see that need to change back to their originality. Think carefully about each development project and carefully analyze its implications.

PEOPLE'S DAILY ACTIVITIES AND CULTURAL BELIEFS

Thinking about the consequences of the actions you put in your time and abilities, the time you are not sure of the whole reason for something, do everything carefully and do it for your good and the good of others. Human activities are not easy for nature; as nature evolves, it will inevitably affect us. On a day-to-day basis, sometimes we find ourselves in a bad situation.

Our blind works allow us to do significant damage, some of which we do to survive and some of which we do by the extreme ignorance of destroying the world in which we live. Gradually, we are contributing to what will happen to us by pretending that we are doing work that will bring us life but soon, we will see the tragedy of our great atrocities. When I look closely, I see that people are destroying the world itself and its inhabitants; this seems to be preparing for an end. What we are planning will ruin the world and burn if we do not change our practices to stop the mistakes of environmental degradation.

We go into the forest to cut it and destroy it so we can get where to cultivate, hunt, live, and exploit the minerals it contains. We deliberately ignore the rain that the forests bring to us, the fresh air they give us, the preservation of the soil from the floodwaters, and the fact that forests are the habitat of other living things that also benefit us, and we destroy them. What plants will we cultivate and keep the soil better than the forest? What minerals will we mine to bring us fresh air?

Tomorrow morning we will say that the rain has stopped, the seasons have changed, and the climate is too hot. The sunny weather will dry up the valleys and the swamps; famine and drought will eventually reach the people. Times like this are tricky because rain can stop for a long time, and when it rains, it brings soil erosion, kills people, and destroys their activities because it no longer controls itself as the forests do, and yet we have made deforestation. The rain will also ruin people's lives through the floods that will destroy people and their livelihoods, and the rest will suffer from severe famine. Therefore, the sun and rain will be trials for us not only when they disappear but also during their vast occurrence. It is unfortunate that as you prepare for the rainy season and be surprised to see that the sun has set without a drop of rain falling, the sun has risen sharply in anticipation of the rain.

So the rainy season also brings changes, and rain brings floods. The floodwaters move everything through the valleys, things get mixed up, and people end up in tears and lose their lives and livelihoods, causing them to starve when they had the chance to survive such a tragedy brought by heavy rainfall. It all ends with a change of season, and sometimes what we do daily brings us more sun and heavy rain, which also results in more damage than before. Then, the time we were ready to cultivate because of the rain that kept the soil was confused with the harvesting period, where the sun dried the plants.

It is unfortunate to hear the elders say that during our times, it was raining, and we were waiting to go to the fields, and again they say that in the past, we used to harvest wheat at that moment. They were cultivating in the past due to the rain, and the sun was average in their occurrence, which allowed the swamps and mountains to have enough water to feed the wheat until they ripened, and the sun would help them harvest promptly.

Disorganization like this causes great hunger because even when you try to cultivate in the hope that the rain will soon disappear, the sun will come in, and the plants will dry up. So the seeds left in the soil waiting for water will be dried, and the solution will be to go and dry the rivers and other water sources to see how we can irrigate the crops until they are ripe. Once cultivation becomes a more demanding profession due to its hard work and low irrigation capacity from the time you plant it to the harvesting time, you would risk and reap the least and low yield compared to the amount of effort used.

In the absence of the sun, heavy rains cause erosion, which destroys the natural vegetation and manure; this leaves behind a void that also causes severe damage. It will also be difficult to cultivate. Where it is possible to produce, it will require fertilizer and irrigation so the cultivation investment will be expensive, and food security will be a severe problem.

Based on what I have just written, you may be wondering about the incredible ignorance of those who burn down forests and kill wildlife to find farms and what they burn to make manure that is too short-lived. Many do not think of others who will follow in the next generation. Still, they enjoy the benefits of short-term productivity and are deceived by the fact that they know they will not live on earth for long and then destroy the environment for a better life. Yet, their descendants are the ones who will be badly affected by what their ancestors did.

It is essential to monitor every action we take, to determine the value and implications for our future. Avoid dumping waste everywhere because it will pollute the environment in which you live. Cleanliness in your body, cleanliness in your home and place of work, cleanliness in your area, and cleanliness in your city or village; shortly hygiene as a culture for the scattered citizens around the world will also reduce environmental pollution.

If we have parted ways from the jungle as the solution and left it entirely to the rest of the wildlife we have left behind, we also need to change the current culture of deforestation for habitation and hunting. Eating animals will make you learn to consume them, thinking that the importance of animals is not only to provide meat but also to preserve them as our future sustenance and avoid misuse. As a person, you should first know that the world is yours and be aware of your actions because if not, we humans will bring an end to the world.

We also need to monitor the current situation, so we do not have to worry about the future. We should pay attention to the important lesson of our experiences of wastage and misuse.

MISUSE AND WASTING OF RESOURCES

The most important lesson people need to learn is to be careful and protect the environment; know how to make the best use of their natural resources because trying to change them a little bit to the environment is detrimental. We also need to avoid misuse and waste that allows us to exploit the natural resources God has given us to control.

Humans need to differentiate themselves from other animals, recognize our basic needs and naturally find and see them at the level of expected survival. For example, it is not good to always eat meat as you need; it will push you to hunt animals to a higher level and make them disappear, and generations that will follow will lack fish because you have become accustomed to eating meat for a long.

That should also be the case for all of our livestock, birds, or landfills; we need to ensure that we do not lose our livelihoods because of our wastage behaviors. If you have harvested fruits or vegetables, be sure to reap what is necessary to be enough, not waste. All the debris is damaging and polluting; eventually, the waste will also inevitably damage us sooner or later. After all, overeating or overdrinking is all about the insanity that leads to less intelligent mistakes that a wise person cannot make, including environmental damage.

Above all, eating fish should not cause us to drown in the sea so that we can eat them and be satisfied by them to the fullest, as if we will not need fish in the future. The good thing is that a balanced meal needs to be mixed with other plants meant to feed the people. It would be best if you ate what makes you think positively, which is the wisdom of better use of resources without waste.

God has promised that all human livelihoods will be helpful when combined in all their categories. Here, it is because all foods you know are not suitable when taken in large quantities and often unless one is compatible with the other for the same benefits that complement each other to provide life.

Above all, we must understand that God's creations were created differently from other creatures to make them useful in their place. So the unity in its value joins with one another to help in human sustenance and nature conservation. Things become too bad when a person takes some species as of little importance; this becomes the beginning of a sense of self-worth and destroys some of them by mistake, and then the necessary compatibility is compromised, and now the consequences begin to creep in from then on. To hear this, you have to wonder what may happen when you kill all the cats. But, of course, there will be many rats, and they will do a lot of damage to the environment as a result of losing their predators.

There is a lot of air pollution that we know is coming from cars and other petrol derivatives, but we often use them daily, even if it is unnecessary. For example, take a walk and leave the car because you know that the exhaust gasses are harmful. It will also save money from wasting fuel and keeps you healthy. The previously mentioned, too, should not be trivial to us; it should always be close to us; however, it can harm us anytime without leaving the environment.

As much as you have the ability, it is not good that you own expensive and useless things so that the public will know that you have money, yet some of them will grow old and become waste without any use except to degrade the environment. But if it helps to protect the environment, you have to buy it as long as you buy it for the poor people who cannot afford it.

People should learn to sacrifice and not waste what God has created to sustain us; we should do it often, especially for the necessary things we see which does not damage the environment. Indeed, we have to use everything to the fullest without showing waste that causes people to destroy the source of their livelihood. For example, if we are looking for fish, we must know that we will need them again and again. That will help us to avoid drought in the oceans, rivers, and lakes to save fish for our future and to protect the next generation.

Also, if we need to eat meat, we should do it in moderation so that tomorrow we will get all the quantity and quality to sustain us. It also makes us aware of the survival of these living creatures that give us such kinds of food. We must fight for them because they are the source of our lives. Therefore, we need to find and prepare enough food to survive, not waste them, because waste pollutes the environment.

It is good to think about the future of the millennium that welcomes us and learns from the mistakes that have been made so that we can correct what is happening to us and take care of ourselves and build a better future. After all, for humans to protect the world, they should respect the other living beings in the ecosystem.

GENERAL ADVICE TOWARD BIODIVERSTY

Embracing biodiversity is life. Yes, we humans are in the world, but we are not alone because we are surrounded by many living and non-living things. The difference starts between a living thing and a non-living thing. For example, a living being characterized by breathing is where we humans belong; but it also includes several classes of organisms with similar characteristics to the unit. Non-living things have natural things such as water, air, and others and artificial stuff like clothes and other materials, all of which vary in their values up to the specific value of the unit.

A person could understand the difference between living beings and non-living things and think there is no connection, yet the strange thing is that the breaths need non-living air to breathe. All living things, whether in water, on land, or flying in the air, need water to survive. This means that living things need to embrace non-living things because they give life to them.

Unit isn't enough in diversity, but its role should be respected to maintain life. In variety, we should know something of great value in providing healthy and long-term vitality. Undoubtedly and logically, members of the living thing category should love each other because they share some traits. Combining the purpose of knowing and preserving the inanimate would become the purpose of spirituality. In the ecosystem, man controls everything around him in all species. One should know and respect the importance of each in giving life. It seems impossible for man to live without plants or other animals in all their species.

From the fish of the Mediterranean Sea to the giant tree in the Amazon forest, from unicellular organisms like bacteria to large animals like elephants; whether aquatic or flying in the air, each has particular importance in nature conservation to sustain life on earth. It all ends up being the person with the most benefit because they all combine in their classification to provide a complete meal that feeds a person.

Every creature has something that makes it different from another. Humans may show little or noticeable difference from other living beings, yet everything defines life. It is good to be included in living things, but no living thing should ignore that life comes from air, water, and the sun, which is included in non-living creatures.

Actually, the difference doesn't matter, but man brought competition and started destroying other organisms to find a breeding ground. This is how plants and animals began to be endangered, and micro-organisms began to live and inhabit humans. The effect is to fill the world with people with short life expectancies. Of course, destroying the forests and damming the rivers so that people can live leads to the disappearance of our sustenance like oxygen and water. Yet it is clear that non-livings will remain even afterlife when living things are gone.

We will never be able to learn the lesson of living well as long as we do not know the importance of the other creatures around us. Again, this is where we have to start because there is a clear difference between humans and other creatures; a person is indeed different from water or air, but if you separate a person from one of them (water or air), a person would not be a person. In the text above, I have shown that man is made up of more water than other things; this is the truth that there is no life in a person when there is no water in it. But look at how much damage we're doing when we try to use toxic bombs, and this makes the water useless for living things.

Even research shows that water is decreasing in the atmosphere due to hydrogen loss to space. Yes, it takes a lot of time, but it is gradual due to human activity. Scientists say that the ocean's water has decreased by a quarter in modern times. Downsizing is a serious problem even though it takes a very long time; I want to ask ourselves, "Is the water around you has the quality to give life?"

Recently and even today, people have polluted water because of their actions; many water pollutants come from human activities, such as sewage and industrial waste. These concentrated pollutants will immediately cause disease and kill any organism in the water or any organism that drinks the water; think of people trying to try bombs in the sea and aquatic organisms suffering physical injuries or dying.

Other pollutants reduce the oxygen in the water, and the oxygen is lost, leading to marine life's anaerobic death. Other substances indirectly pollute the water, making the water unhealthy and not conducive to health. The worst thing is that water pollution, like organic waste, pesticides, poisonous and explosive substances, fertilizers, and heat, is all the result of human activities. Therefore, we should protect water from anything that could harm it because if we don't, we will harm ourselves.

I'm trying to show you the big mistakes we're making that will ruin our future because we don't know how to deal with biodiversity. Imagine that we are destroying the air breathed by living things, even though we people use that air. But every time we raise more smoke in the air, it causes a reaction that will result in the formation of greenhouse gases.

Consider also the emissions from many development activities; Industries that emit fumes into the atmosphere, sometimes even make other products that will pollute the air we breathe. The more we compete in development, the more we are in a race to destroy the environment, and the most developed are the ones who led others in polluting, but we will share the negative consequences.

Do you ever wonder about nuclear weapons factories; in the process of making these weapons, there is incredible destruction, whether it is the destruction of nature or the atmosphere, but the most unfortunate thing is that the resulting weapon will destroy people and things, destroy everything they have achieved.

This damage reaches other living things even though we don't really care about it; what I want to say is that the explosion of these bombs raises tons of harmful gases that will do more damage to the atmosphere than the damage they are currently doing. But can't we people at least agree to hold back and deal with the consequences of past mistakes? Do nuclear bombs really make you feel safe? On the contrary, I can see that you are always afraid of a madman who will come out of you and do atrocities you have never seen and imagined before.

But, of course, we are worried about it; not only will it blow us to death because we won't live forever, but its consequences will make the world worse in the future and harm natural life until human beings disappear. Let us accept that the factory would send smoke into the air, but at least they are making bread or clothes, but it is sad to see that the factories are polluting by making more polluting substances.

Think of Joseph, who works in a weapons factory. This story started when Joseph was indeed unemployed. He received an offer for a vacant position in a certain factory to replace an employee who was killed by explosive substances in the factory. Fortunately, he applied, was shortlisted, and passed all the written exams and the interview. However, when he was going to start, they told him the work instructions included always wearing full-person protective equipment that covers the whole body.

The manager said, "Listen, Joseph, the deceased worked here for two years and was found guilty of not complying with these regulations".

Manager added, "We are a great company because we have many awards and certificates. However, I guess you have seen that we make weapons; here, there are explosive chemical substances that kill, including bad air that you cannot breathe to live; you will not eat anything in this work; you should take care of it".

He was given many other instructions that would help him in his work. Joseph calmly replied, "Yes, I heard that, but don't you offer life insurance? I think someone may have a problem at work because there are a lot of risks here".

The manager laughed, "You ask an excellent question; we provide insurance, and you will see it in the contract you will sign. Joseph, you are now our permanent employee because you will be out of a job when you die, we will give you the possible security to keep you safe, and it is easy because we give you a house to live near the workplace."

Joseph looked like someone who doesn't want to talk anymore but says, "I will read the contract carefully; I think I will find everything in it, but if I may ask again, why are you offering all those? I mean the permanent contract, the house, and the security you provide; why else?"

The manager said, "Well, here we use strict confidentiality; we don't want anyone, including our competitors, to know our operations and plans. Also, we must protect you because there are criminals outside the company and others who bought guns here; Joseph, they can rob you or kill you when you return home from work."

"I understand you've thought about what's best for your employees, but is there a planned vacation? I'm talking about leaving the confines of the company, and one can travel to a place in the beautiful nature, where one can see animals and relax. Does the manager have such a plan?" Joseph claimed.

The manager sadly replied, "We do this once in three months; however, the park we used to visit has been badly damaged due to the war in that country; the information I have is that bombs have burned the forest and the animals are dying." Here he was referring to a part of Africa where there are armed groups. He added:

"Well, there are various beautiful places, but there is always war; we plan to take the workers to the beaches of the eastern seas of the world."

Joseph defended him, saying, "That can be possible; the problem is that I read the news that the water there is not so good that people can swim in it." The story was about how the water was contaminated due to the testing of highly toxic explosives. "Manager, let's leave, you know, I will start work tomorrow; let's stop this trip topic because even the place I was thinking about there is a serious epidemic," Joseph suggested.

"That's it, there are currently rumors that epidemics come from human activities, I don't know; let's get to work and thank you, Joseph, and you showed me confidence in being a good employee. I believe that together we will reach the goal of making the first bomb in the world so that even its fumes alone can kill the enemy," the Manager hardly said.

"See you, boss," Joseph concluded, "I saw that you are qualified to work with us; then see you at work, Mr. Joseph," Manager replied.

The story above is not a testimony of what actually happened, but I intend to show you the consequences of what we do willingly or blindly. Humans have made many mistakes, but our conflicts have greatly impacted other species, causing them to die in large numbers and others to disappear completely. Now we come to the time of correcting the errors by other errors and in a non-stop manner. I tell you the truth; if you put on a scale to weigh the efforts put into preserving the environment and the efforts put into destroying it, you will find that destruction is our priority; you can think people are tired of the world and want to end it.

Why else should we embrace biodiversity? I have said many times in my writings that our existence is due to other natural beings, whether animate or inanimate. For example, I explained the importance of water and air, trying to show how they contribute to human beings. But also remember that all food consists of plants and the meat of other animals. Therefore, biodiversity is vital, and people should permanently conserve biodiversity.

Each of these networks has its own role, whether it's in what we eat or don't eat. Everything is a chain because what a person does not eat is eaten by other animals that a person consumes; this makes everything to be respected in the ecosystem. It should also be understood that healthy eating is the conservation of biodiversity; the reason is that it requires a person to eat different types of food on average, which leads to harm to no single species from regularly consuming the same kind of food alone.

The amazing thing is that our tendency to eat one thing pushes us to harm and ends up being self-destructive; After all, one thing does not provide a balanced diet.

After all, eating itself because one is hungry cannot harm nature; instead, greed causes others to lack food and damage the environment. Look at the destruction of living things because of war, yet they don't kill animals or destroy the environment because they want to eat, nope, but they hunt people to kill them and cause them to do more damage. Well, that's why hunting becomes a problem because the hunter wants to eat only meat, causing many animals to die, so people don't have a sustainable future balanced diet. The other thing is that it forces them to destroy other organisms by burning them to find prey

So would you take care of the environment without knowing its importance? You should first know the role of water, air, light, plants, animals, and other living things in making life possible.

CONCLUSION

It's great that you've reached the end of this book; I'm glad you're going to use the lessons you've learned to change your community. That is how people should live well with biodiversity so that there are no activities that people do that lead to the destruction of the environment, which results in climate change.

Without a doubt, the current climate change is because people did not value the environment; we have seriously damaged the ecosystem due to our development activities that have made us ignore the importance of other creatures in nature conservation. We cut down the forests, dammed up the rivers and swamps, and exploited the mountains; we do everything to find how to build beautiful houses, even to find precious stones and petroleum extraction; yet none of these give health like water or provide fresh air like forests.

Embracing biodiversity, it is the best advice because it prevents harming the environment because one knows the importance of things in the environment. Always try to befriend diversity in every possible way; if a person knows the value of something, one takes care of it, embraces and protects it. In ecosystem, there is not a single creature without value and many creatures exist to make human live. That is why a man was created after all other creatures.

REFERENCES

1. Petry, Walter. (2021). Origin and Evolution of the Universe. Journal of Modern Physics. 12. 1749-1757. 10.4236/jmp.2021.1213102.
2. Padhy, Chitrasena & Kalee, Prasanna & Pattanayak, Kalee & Reddy, M. & Kumar, Rabindra & Anusandhan, Siksha. (2022). Biodiversity-An Important Element for Human Life.
3. Change, Intergovernmental. (2022). Climate Change and Land: IPCC Special Report on Climate Change, Desertification, Land Degradation, Sustainable Land Management, Food Security, and Greenhouse Gas Fluxes in Terrestrial Ecosystems. 10.1017/9781009157988.

THANK YOU!

LET'S MEET IN THE NEXT BOOK!

www.ingramcontent.com/pod-product-compliance
Lightning Source LLC
Chambersburg PA
CBHW061513250726
48657CB00005B/1840